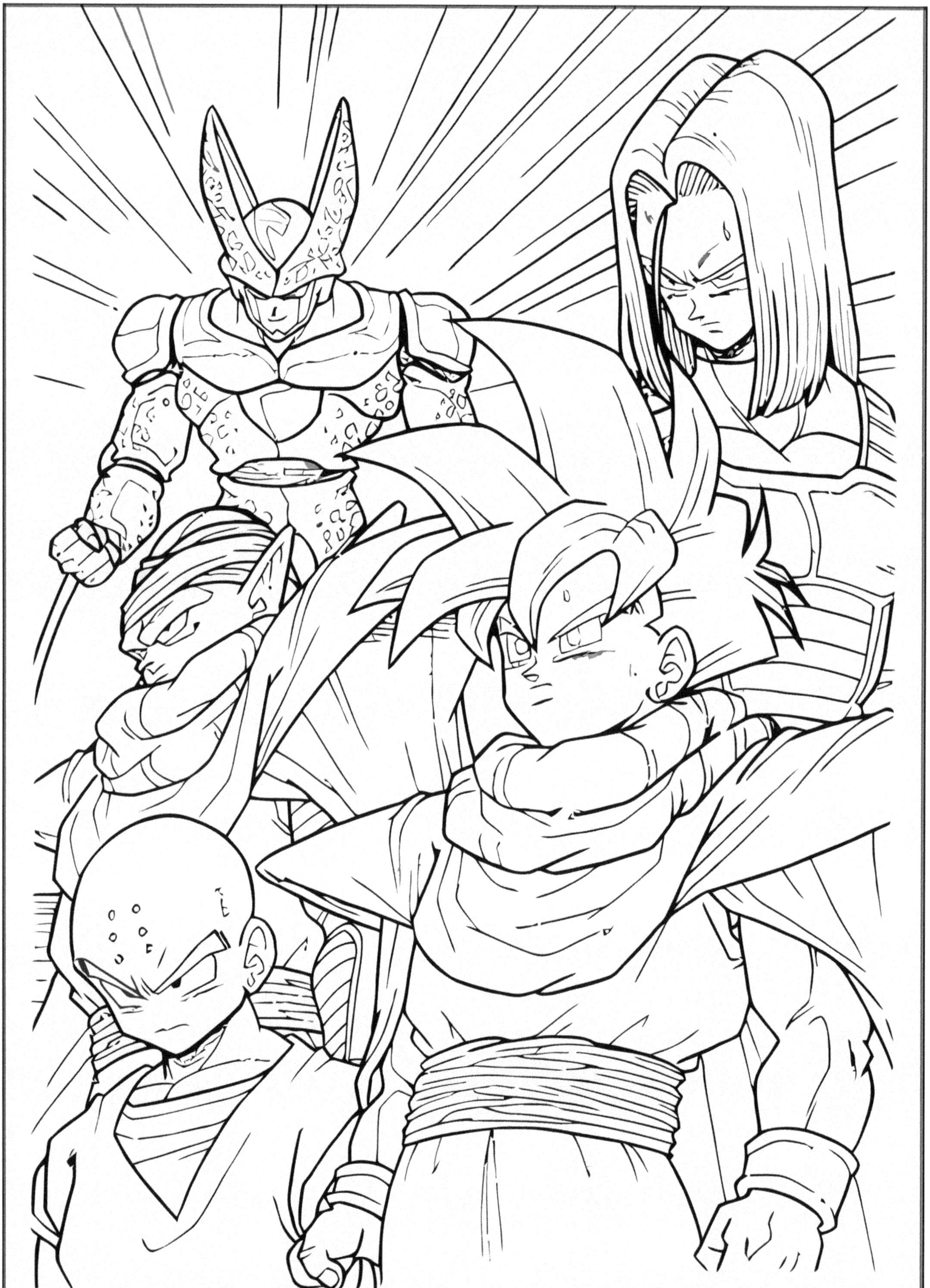

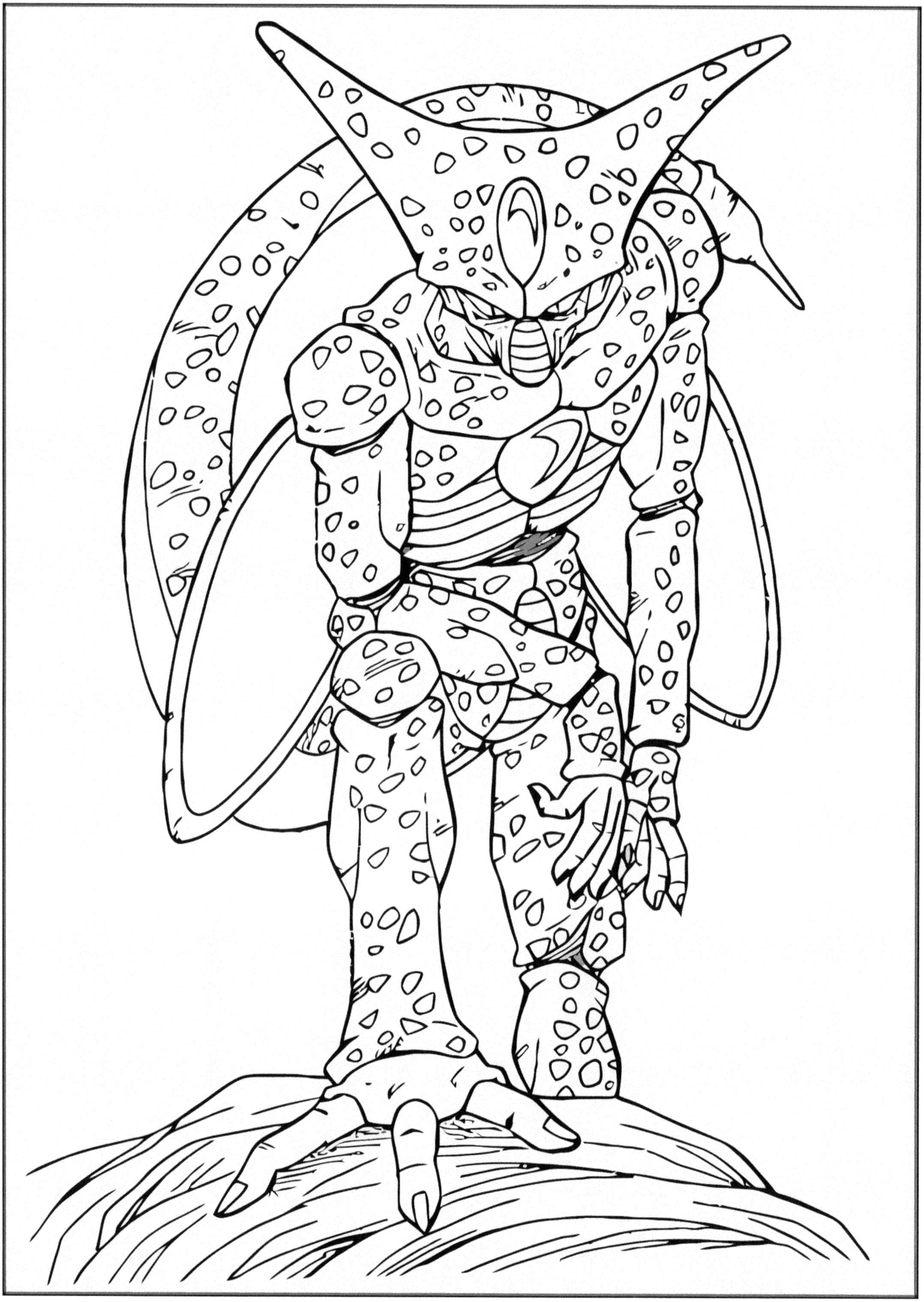

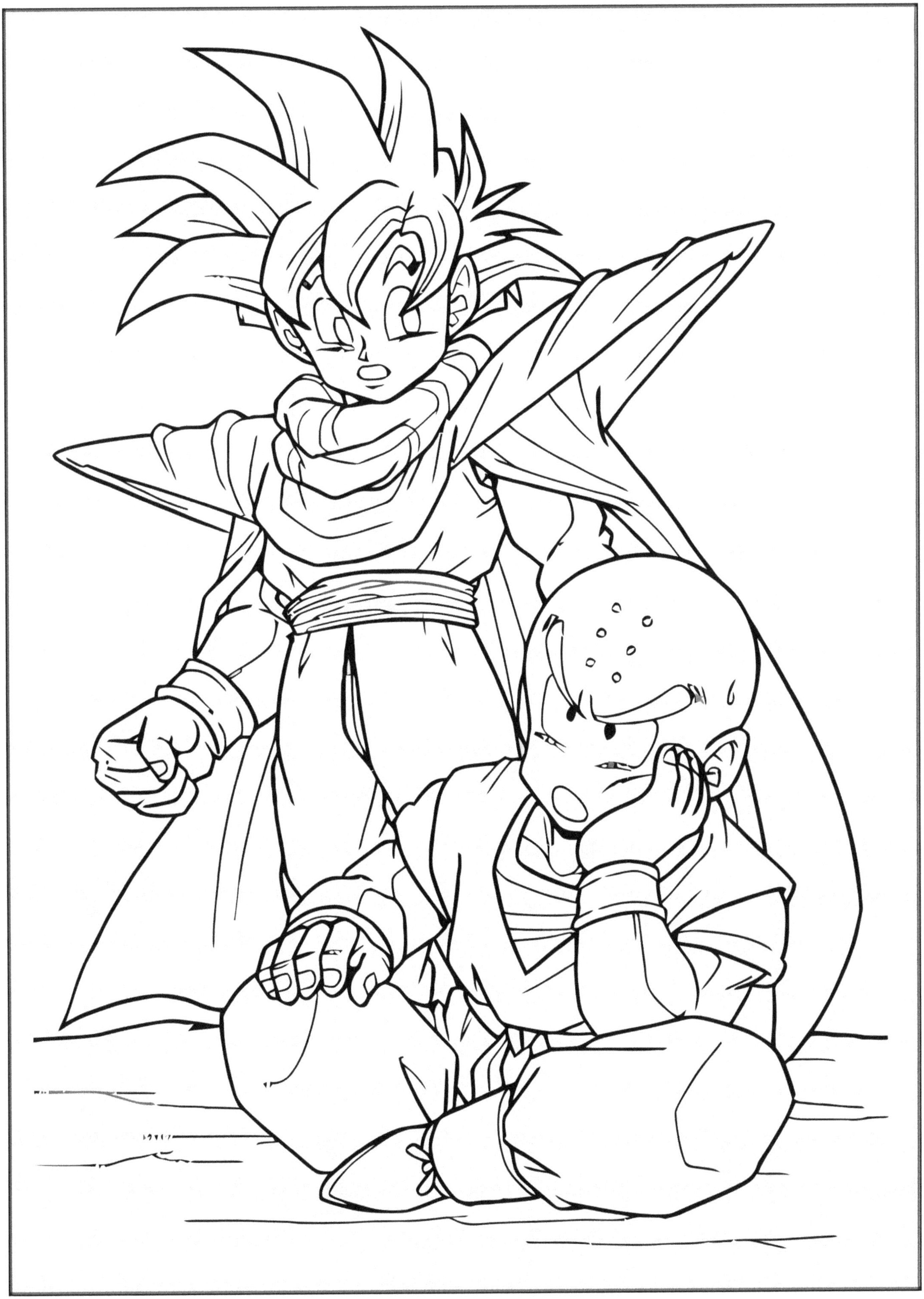

神

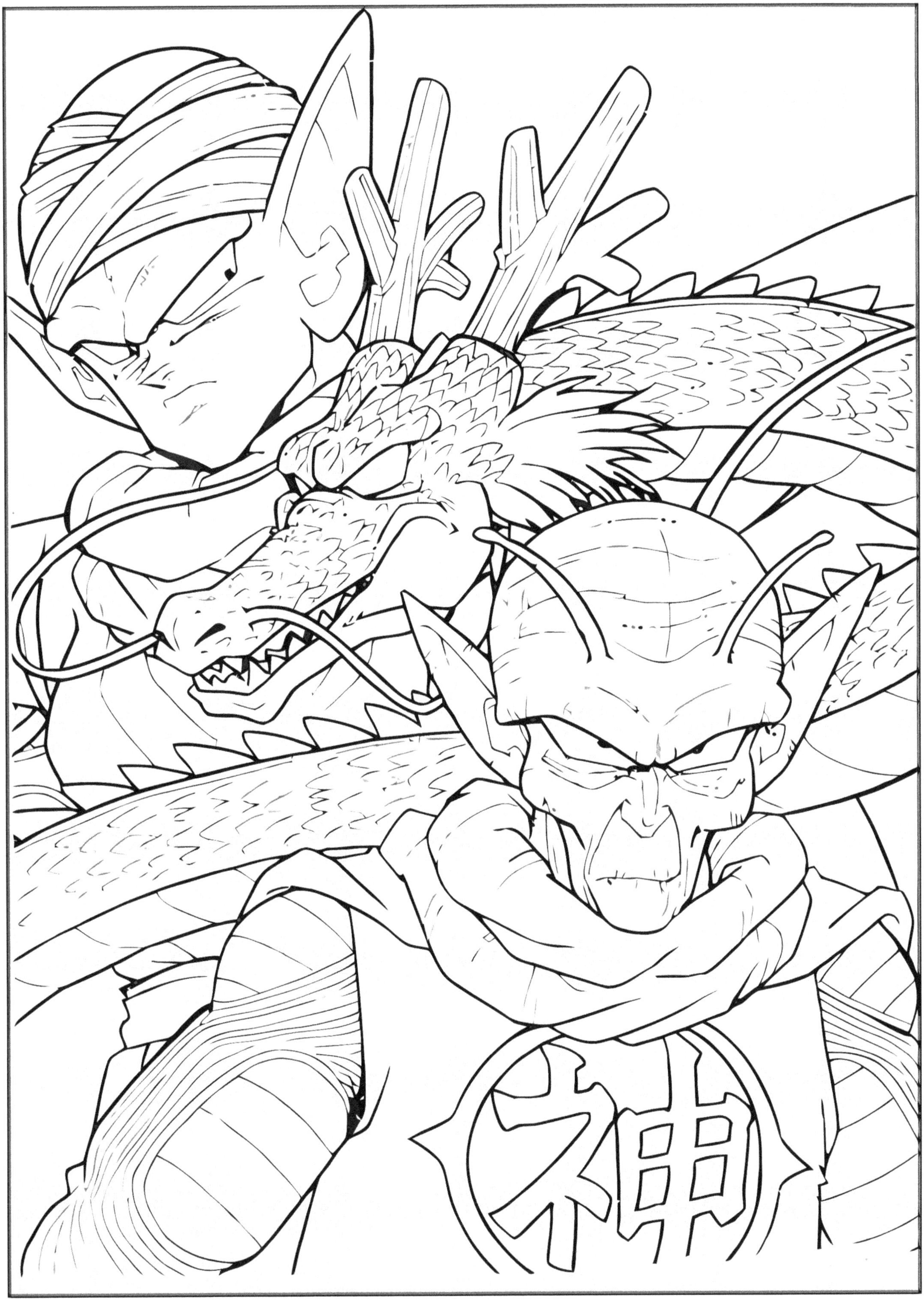
神

亀

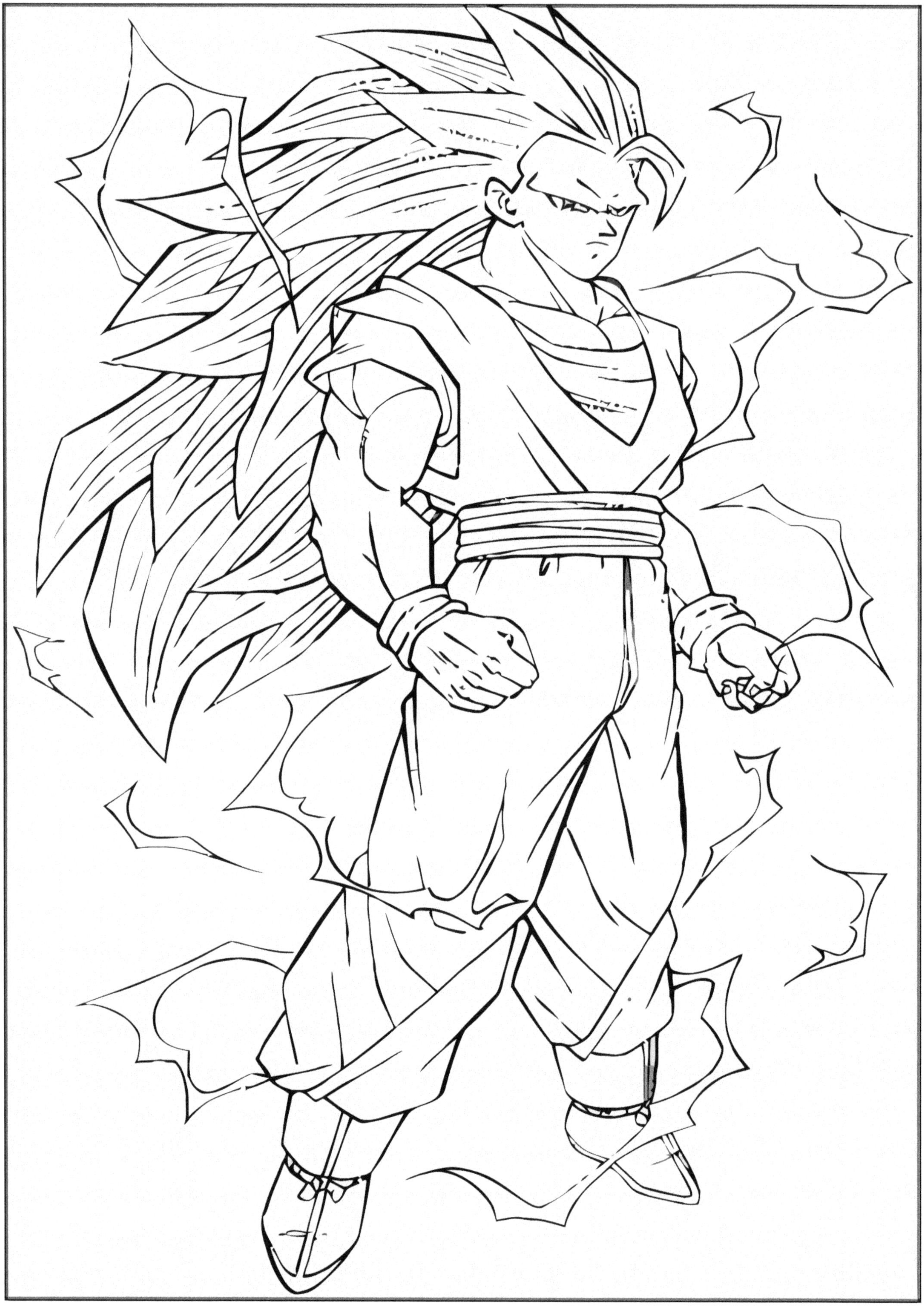

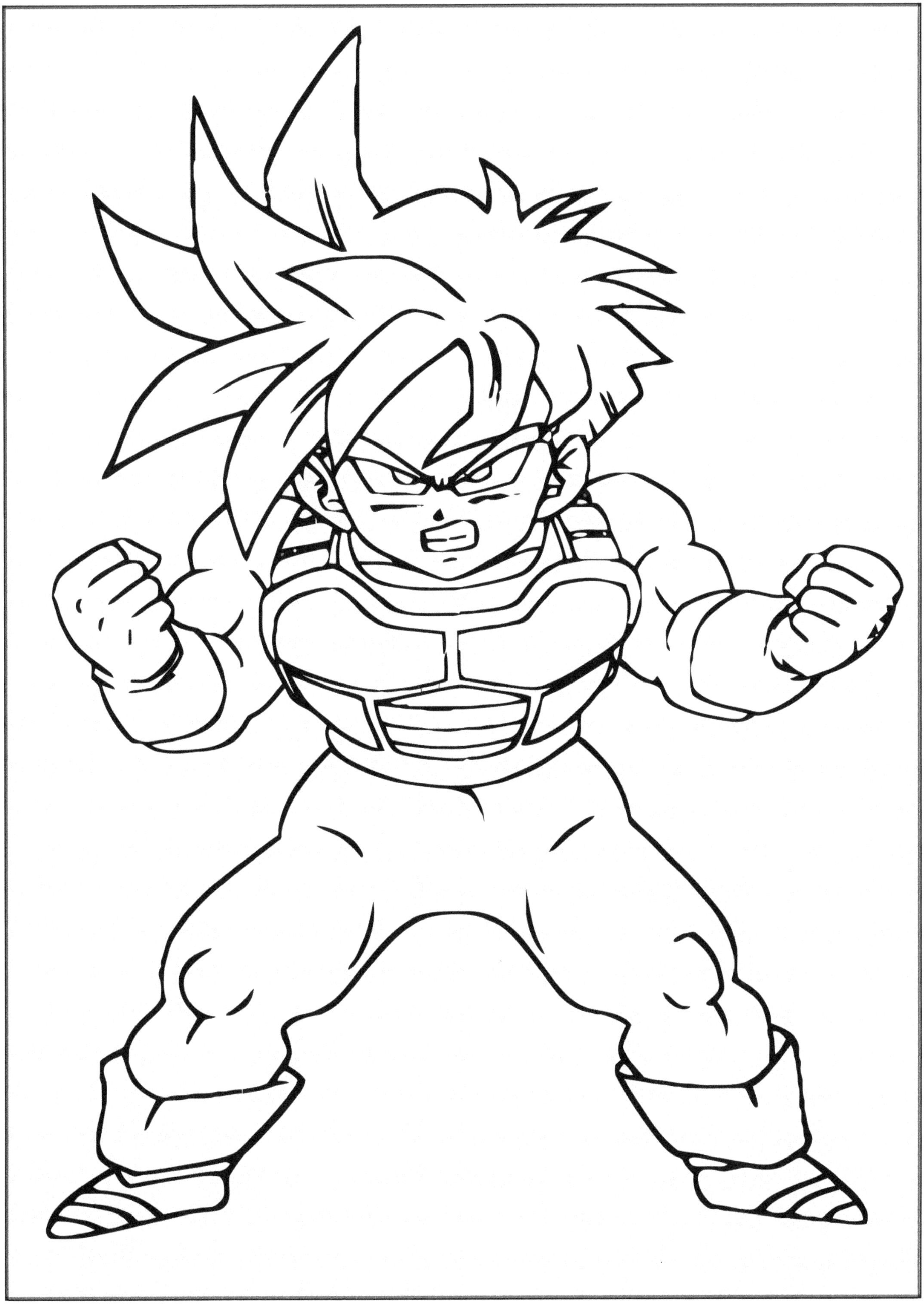

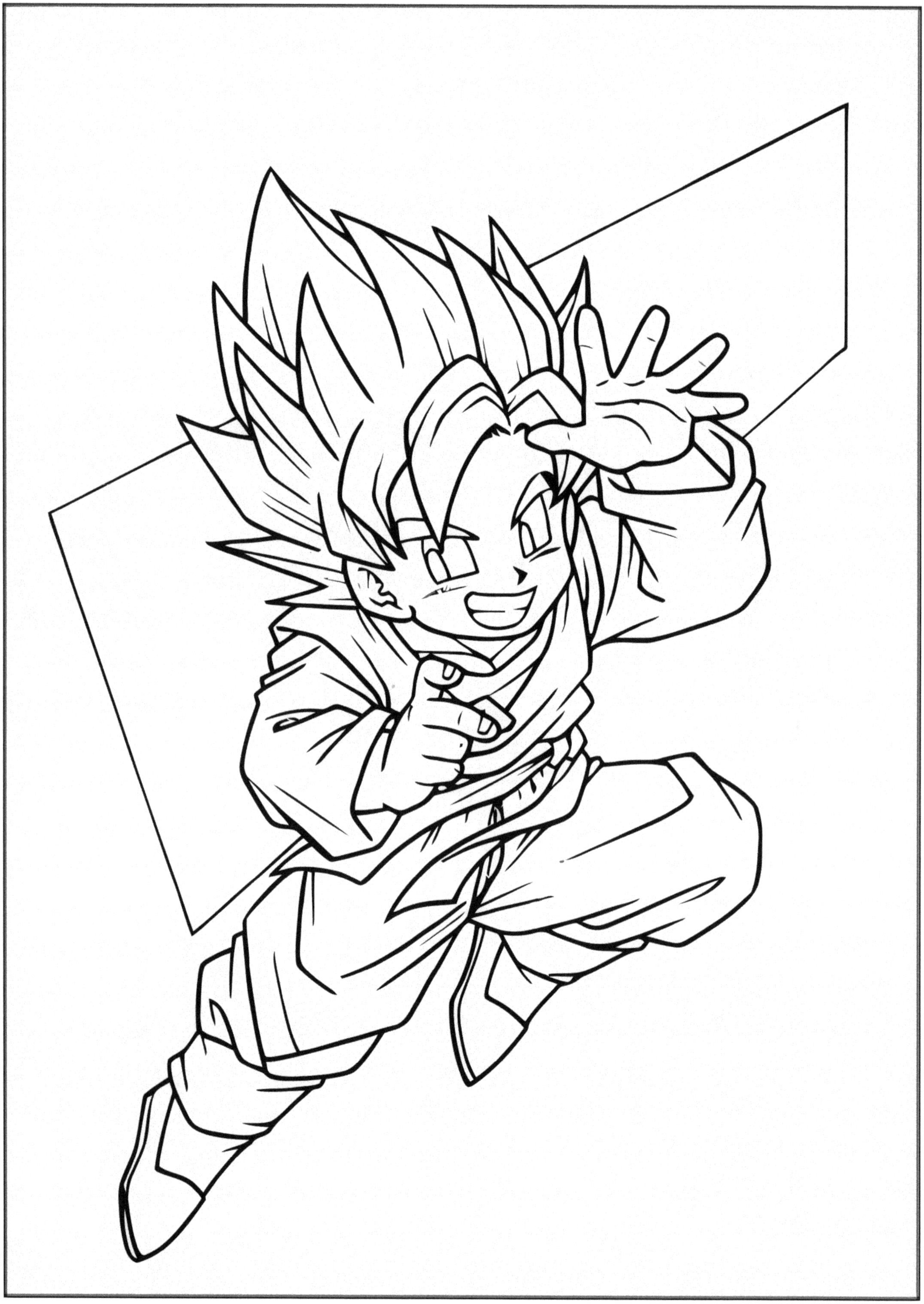

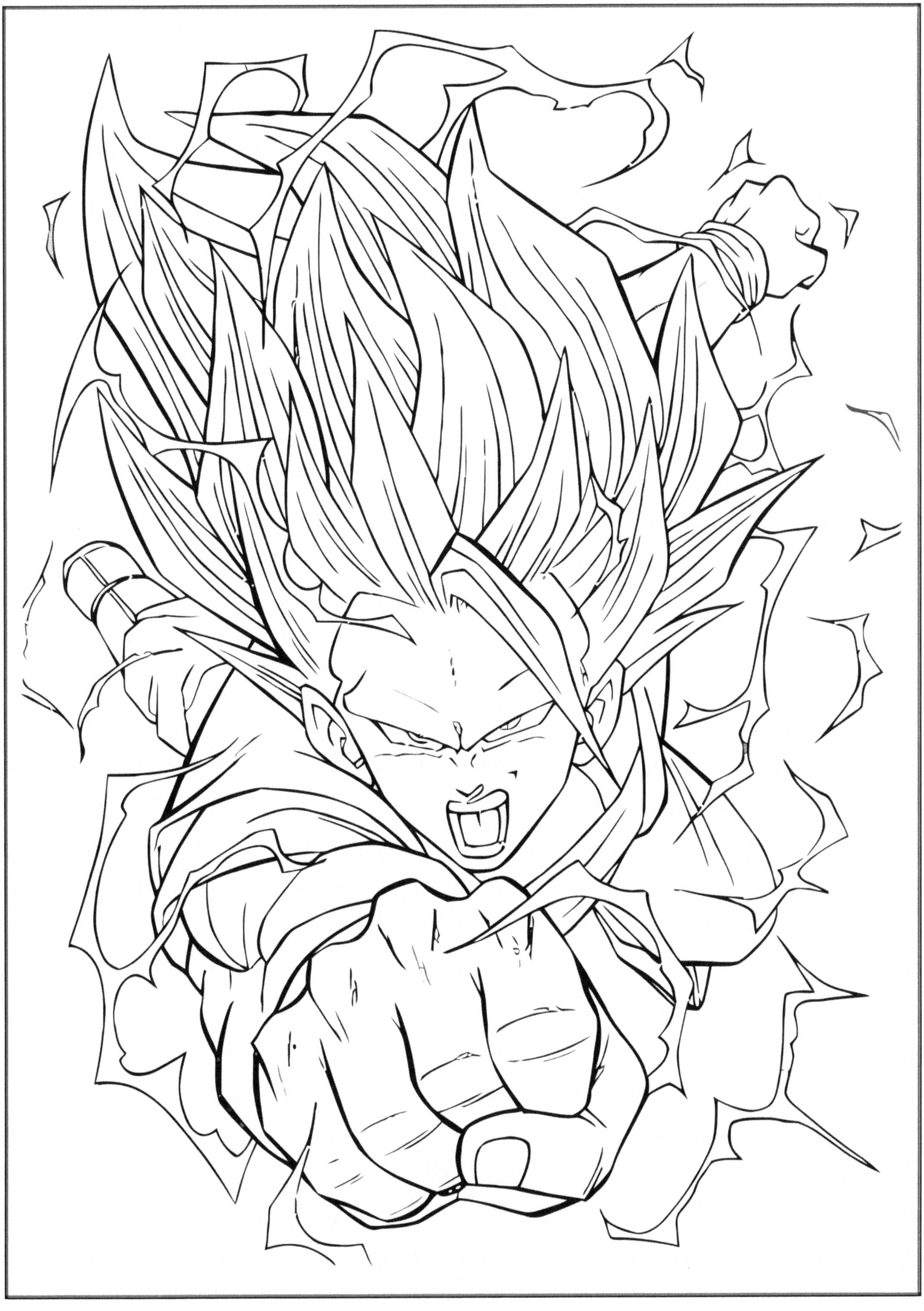

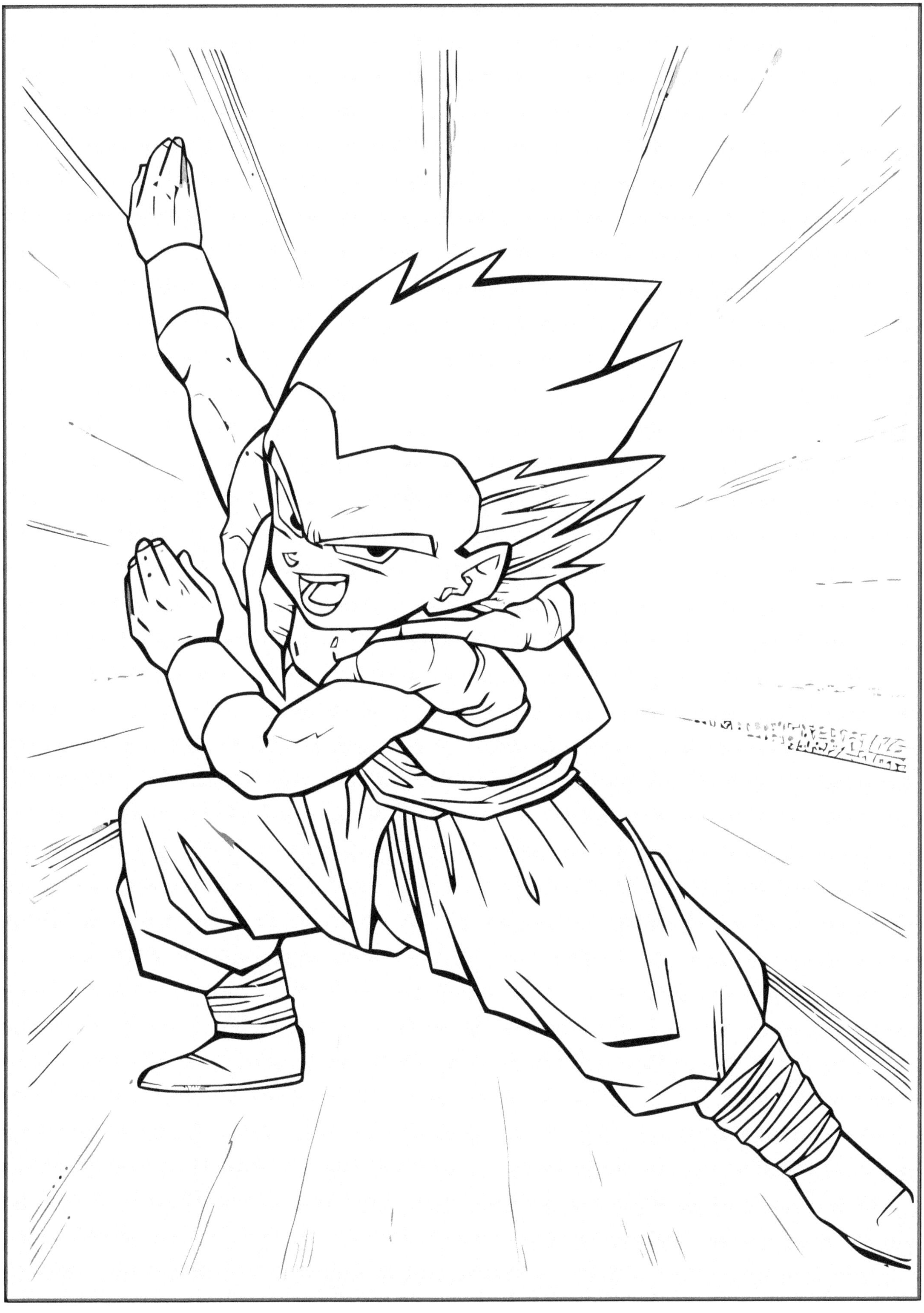

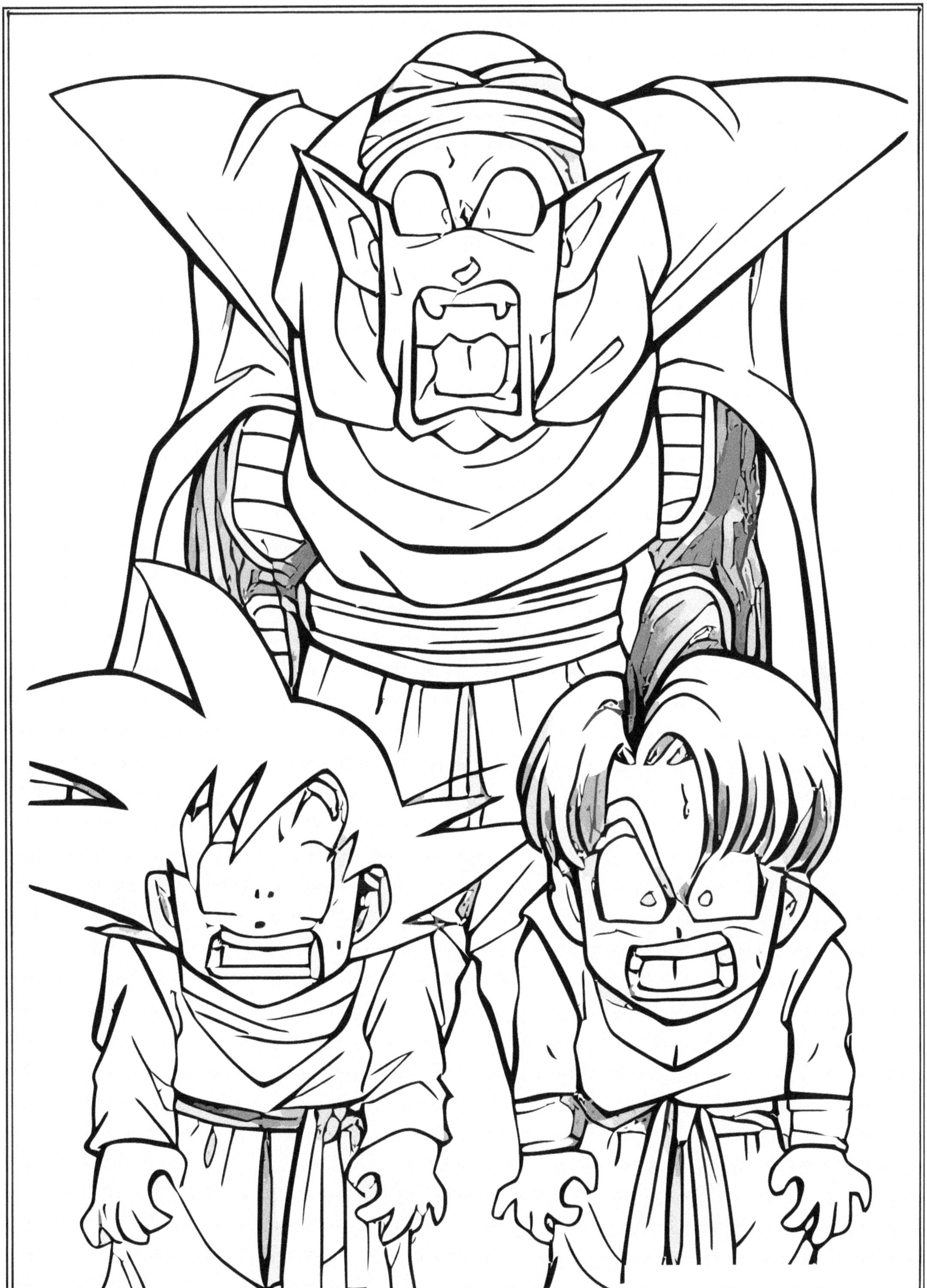

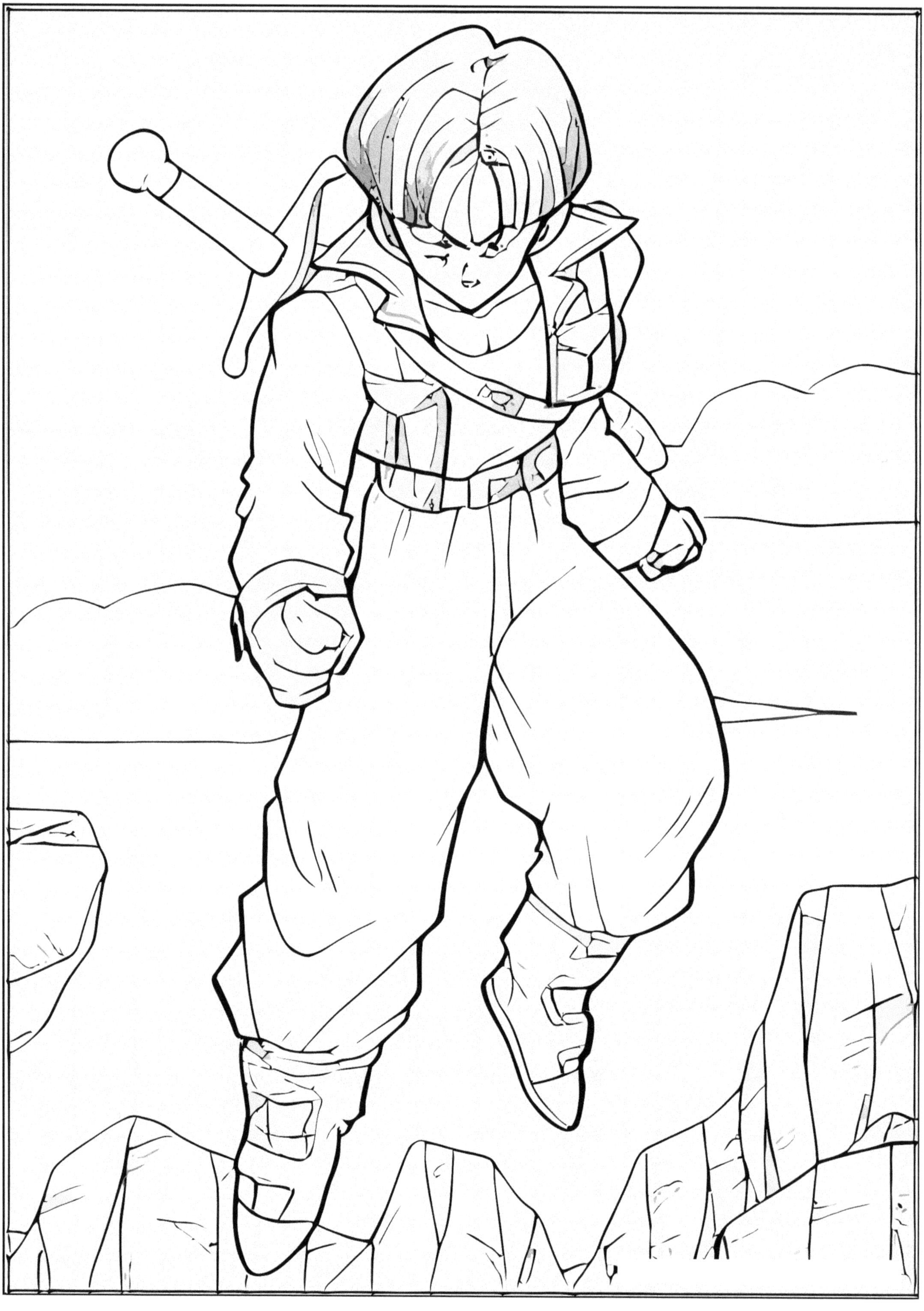

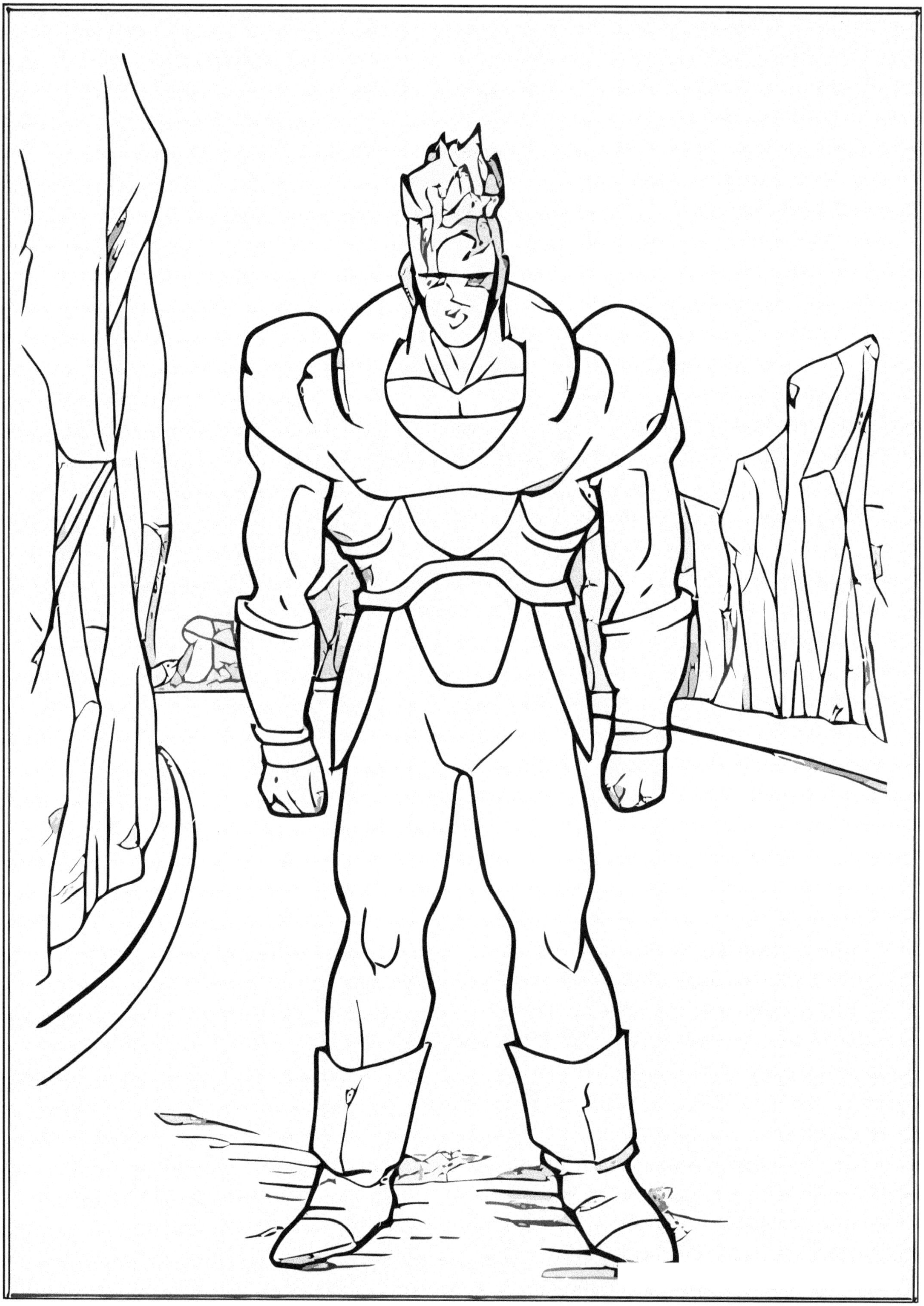

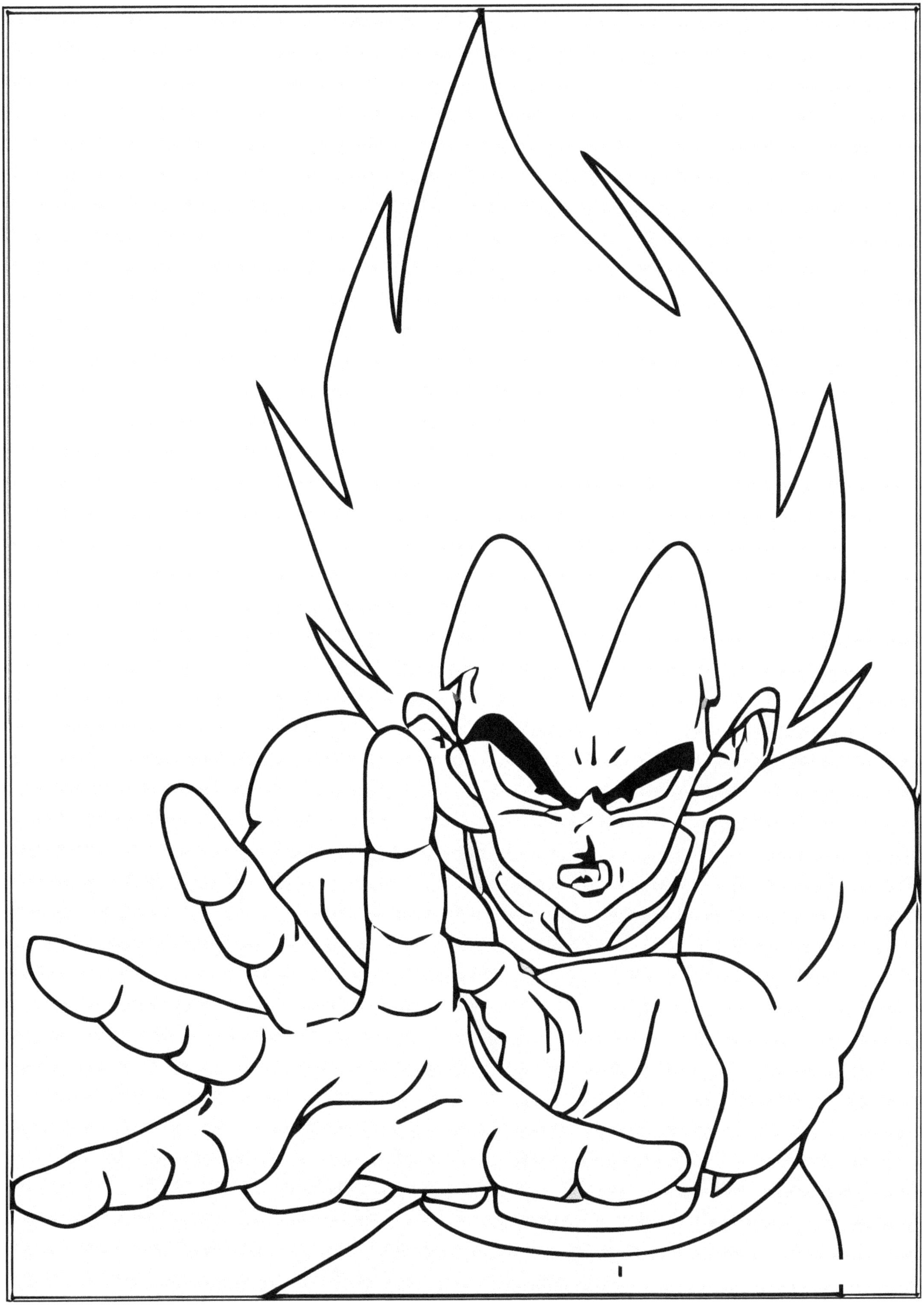

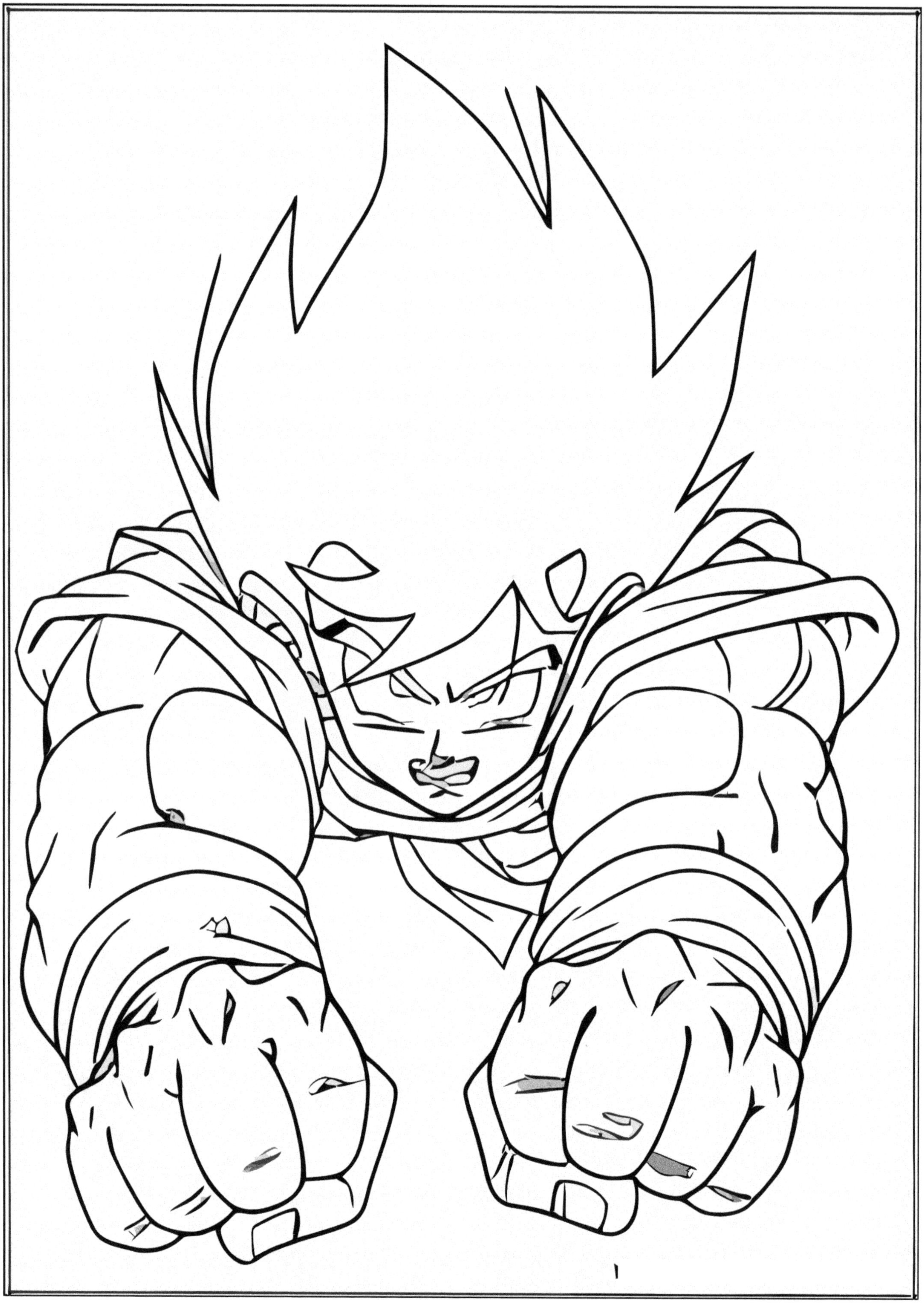

トランクス

Printed in the USA
CPSIA information can be obtained
at www.ICGtesting.com
LVHW060800201124
797039LV00018B/354
9782389239424